COME BE COZY

by jennae cecelia

COME BE COZY

come be cozy

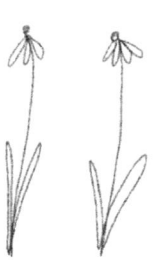

come be cozy is filled with poems about the journey of self-love and relationships. along with words that make you feel nostalgic and think about your life and all that is happening around you. it is a poetry book to find comfort in and shed a tear or two. light a candle, grab a blanket, brew some tea, and turn the pages.

come be cozy

it is cozy here

will this be the year?
i'm not really sure.
i only know for certain
what is happening right now.
that my coffee tastes perfect.
the sunlight is flooding the kitchen
with golden beams.
my friend just texted me a book
she thinks i should read.
and it might not seem like much,
but it's now.
and that's everything.

maybe today is your birthday.
and times have changed.
you no longer need
the gifts or the cake.
instead of waiting around
for a happy birthday text that truly lacks,
your significant other wakes you up
singing happy birthday and you laugh.
you go out for pastries and coffee.
find a comfy new sweater at the store.
you write in your journal
about the year to come and the year before.
maybe birthdays look different now,
but it is all you could have ever hoped for.

i want takeout sushi with you.
a glass of red wine or two.
i drip the soy sauce.
i spill the wine.
you wipe it away
and chuckle that it's fine.
we clink together the antique glasses
i found at goodwill.
my lipstick staining the side of the glass.
i want to enjoy these small simple
moments with you,
because the present is all we have.

i no longer surround myself with people
that when i tell them all i love,
they tell me why they hate
those same things so much.

i will pick flowers
to put on the table.
light a candle.
set the mood.
but it is not what you think.
it is for me
not for you.
but feel free to enjoy it
for yourself too.

you go for a picnic in the park.
pack martinis and stay until it is dark.
the candles don't stay lit because of the wind.
but you aren't even noticing.
your eyes only on him.
he burned you a CD like it is 2003.
the songs he wants you to listen to feel at ease.
he puts his hand on your knee.
goosebumps on your body
start to show.
thank god the candles won't stay lit.
but it doesn't matter because
in the stars you glow.

it's sunday.
your mom calls.
she tells you she misses
hearing your voice.
you let her know
you only have a moment to talk.
she whispers, *"ok."*
telling you stories about her week,
but knows you are only half listening.
you are in a rush.
she tells you she misses you so much.
you say that you miss her too.
but you say it at a quick pace
and she recognizes she is disturbing you.
she says she will call you again next week.
you tell her ok and you hear her sigh in defeat.
but you are in a hurry
and don't have time to stop and ask if she is ok.
it is sunday again years from now.
your life has slowed down.
you pick up the phone and it rings.
your daughter answers and tells you
she is just getting ready to leave.
can she call you next week?
you tell her ok in a soft voice.
and right before she hangs up,
you let her know you miss hearing her voice
and how you regret the time
you spent in a rush.
that you would do anything to hear
your mother's voice on a sunday again.
she pauses for a moment and says,
"ok mom i am listening.
tell me how you have been."

i want breakfast in the morning with you.
as i make the toast a little too burnt.
you laugh but say it's nothing butter can't fix.
we cheers our coffee in mugs
i made at a free pottery class in town,
and they drip a little out the bottom.
you laugh but say
the coffee tastes better out of it.
and it's comfy.
and it's cozy.
and it's a little bit messy.
and it's all i have dreamed of how
my mornings with you would look.

you welcomed me in through the front door.
you were the first to do this to me.
the last guy told me to call when i was there.
come through the fence and backyard.
asked if anyone saw me.
i would say no.
he would let out a sigh of relief.
but now with you, the windows are wide open.
you kiss me as i come in.
you don't worry about who is seeing us
and who isn't.

i am afraid of the ocean,
but i will swim in it with you.
you make me forget the fears i have,
because i know i am safe in your hands.

i loved people at their darkest,
but oh am i deserving to be
met with light now.
i can only give so much
before i am worn down.

i used to pretend i liked white and cream.
that bright colors in my wardrobe
weren't a need.
but how boring i became
when i tried to dress to appeal
to what other people like.
i am a bright yellow sweater kind of girl.
i no longer care if they think
that is alright.

i'll meet you with tippy toes
on the kitchen floor.
in your t-shirt from the night before.
you'll kiss my forehead.
i'll feel safe.
you made me pancakes
even though i said wasn't hungry.
but you already knew that wasn't true.
and i think in that moment
i fell in love with you.

we go to a fancy restaurant.
the first time in a long time.
we saved up money for that night.
they bring out our order
and i try not to look confused.
there is more plate than food.
the bill comes.
it is $222.
i try not to laugh out of ridiculousness.
you pay the bill
and we quickly exit.
as we get in the car to go home,
you ask me what drive-thru
we are stopping at.
i snort laugh.
and it was truly the best
mcdonald's i have ever had.

you blow the steam
coming off my coffee for me.
always considerate.
i am not used to that.
you keep asking me if i am doing ok.
i am not used to that.
and when i answer yes
you look into my eyes to see
if they are telling another story.
because you care.
oh, do you care for me.

it's a warm summer day.
humidity in the air.
you can tell by my frizzy hair.
you pour us each a glass of lemonade.
freshly squeezed you say.
i laugh a bit,
because i saw
the container from the store in the fridge.
i try not to let my mind wander
to a place of thinking of what else
you could be lying about.
i don't want to ruin this perfect day.
i know there's a difference between
a joke and a lie.
i apologize that my ability
to tell the difference isn't the best.
i have been burned a few times.

the highways get us to places
at a faster pace,
but you need the backroads
and the pit stops to honor yourself.
this season of life is not a race.

it's saturday.
you're at your grandma's.
she asks you if you want to play cards.
you tell her of course.
she makes a pot of coffee.
black.
no sugar or cream.
it tastes like water.
but you smile and sip it anyways.
she tells you about her flowers
growing in the garden.
you listen with so much care.
she comments on the color of your hair.
brown.
like hers used to be.
she asks you if you want coffee.
you say yes, please.
she makes a pot.
no sugar or cream.
she tells you about her flowers.
as she passes the same cards out.
and comments on the brown tone of your hair.
you smile and listen with so much care.
you repeat the process a few more times.
it's saturday at your grandma's
and you don't know if
she has much more time.

i would hand write you love letters.
you couldn't even text me back.
how i thought we would make it,
i will never understand.

you bring me a chocolate donut
with sprinkles.
my favorite kind.
i was craving it last night.
you woke up before me
and snuck out while i slept.
that is what i love most about you.
the small things don't go unnoticed.

the rain falls all around us.
you pull me in.
is this going to be
that cheesy movie scene
where i fall in love with him?
you get close to my lips
and i laugh just a bit.
you twirl me around
and say,
"you are it."
i look at you with contentment in my eyes.
i never thought this would be my life.
i was used to the rain coming from my tears.
but now i am dancing in it
with the man i hold most dear.

i don't need to be popular
or have everyone like me.
i have learned that
a few close friends who know me deeply
means more than a room full of people
who only know me on a surface level.

my past has gotten to the point where
i only remember it in bits and pieces.
through foggy memories.
i am happy because i once relived it in detail.
over
and over
and over again.
telling myself what i should have
done instead.
but the future gave me hope that i could
forgive myself with time.
i no longer feel like a prisoner to
my past self in my mind.

let this year be the one
i do more things for me
and less for the people watching.
no longer apologizing for my quirks.
being last from the table to stand up.
having paint on my hands from a creative session.
asking endless questions.
yes, i will take the whipped cream on my coffee.
i'll probably write you some poetry
and know when the full moon is out.
but i'll love you hard and tell you often.
that is what life is truly about.

i want to be the arms you come running to
when you need to feel safe.
brush your hair out of your face.
tell you it is going to be ok.
but i embrace your cries
because i recognize
that to you it doesn't feel that way.

i lost my story for a little while.
i let someone else write it for me.
now i am taking back
this chapter and the whole book.
ready to tell the world who i am without you.
better.

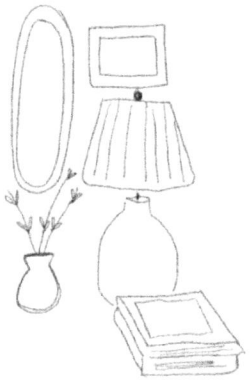

you bring me home
to meet your family for the first time.
the walls are painted white.
it isn't as cozy
as i was told it would be.
a house with white sheets.
beige everything.
you grew up here?
is all i can think.
your mom pours me a glass of red wine.
i fear holding it as i look around
at all i can spill on in sight.
i drink it fast to not have to worry
about dripping it.
your mom looks at me
with slight disapproval on her face.
while asking if she can pour me more.
i say, *"yes please"* and
"can you show me which one
is the bathroom door?"
she points to her left and i hurry right in.
the towels are white too
and there is a bleach scent.
and at that moment i wonder,
can i be perfect and put together
enough for you,
or will i be the mess that comes
crashing through?

and at the end of the day,
it is only myself that can
fully make my life better.
i am the one living in my head.
feeding it sentences
that are either good or bad.
but let's be honest it is hard
to not be your worst critic.

she is beautiful.
summer.
oh, how she glows.
confident in herself.
going where the wind blows.
she will bring out the best in me.
after brutal times.
she is everything i need
to bring me back to life.

one thing about me
is that i remember everything.
details so small
will not go lost in my mind.
i'll remember that friday night
five years ago.
what you wore and how you smelled.
the food we ate.
the walk back to the hotel.
i remember it all.
every detail.
so small.
but if you ask me about it,
i'll pretend i only
vaguely remember a few things.
my mind isn't a place that forgets easily.

she never judged.
only loved.
arms wide open.
making you feel like the only one.
that the world was different because of you.
she was autumn sunsets
and the full moon.
shining light your way
even if she barely knew you.

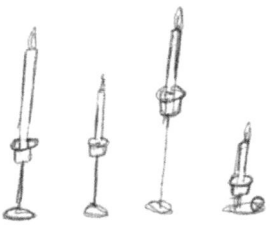

i'm sorry that i was the only one
to say that you are so special.
please don't change.
i can tell you are letting the world
dress you in what pleases them.
but i like you best when you are the one
who picks it out instead.

to be honest,
i wasn't sure about you because
you weren't the safe bet i was used to.
i loved how your hair looked like you always
were playing with the wind
and how you wore yellow so well.
you weren't afraid to laugh really loud
and you called everyone bro.
you had a dandelion tucked behind your ear
for a whole class session
and acted like you didn't know.
and when i asked why you had that ankle tattoo
you said it was because some guy dared you.
and i knew you weren't the safe bet
i was used to.
you were always
pleasantly surprising me
and still do.

i am an old soul.
i love music far before my time.
i go to bed early every night.
i appreciate deep conversations.
i make a home for the blanket
you gave away
that looks like your grandma
spent time to make.
i am an old soul not knowing
how to dance with the new.

i want cozy sweaters
and cinnamon rolls.
i want the air to feel crisp
and to spend some time alone.
i want all things good
for my mental health.
this is the season of
taking care of myself.

how did we go from talking every day
to now just texting each other
on our birthdays?
nothing crazy.
just a simple happy birthday
with a smile.
what happened to the novel we would send
full of love and memories?
this week is my birthday
and i am already dreading you texting me.
because that means i have to face,
that we are no longer friends in the same way.

if i put procrastination to rest
i would have more than half
of my problems solved.
but i like to play this game with myself
where i try to catch myself quick
right before i fall.

you are the moon.
i am the sun.
hardly ever around
at the same time.
my mornings.
your nights.
ships passing.
right person.
wrong time.
i often wonder what would happen if
we got to meet for long.
two lights so bright the world
probably couldn't handle us.

i love the smell of a rainy day.
it feels like my pain
is being washed away.
a chance to start over.
breathe life into what needs to grow.
rainy days are some of the most beautiful.

we go out for a drink.
you tell me you have been
thinking about me all week.
i try not to get too excited.
i have heard this before.
they all love bomb you at first.
and then they start to show
what their true colors were.
we go out for a drink
and i tell myself this time
will be different than i think.

i think about you all of the time.
saturday.
september.
monday.
june and july.
i miss being a part
of every aspect of your life.
but now i text you goodnight
and there is no response.
i feel lost.
i got so wrapped up in you
i forgot about me.
and now i am alone and forgot
how to be in my own company.

you tucked my hair behind my ear
and traced your finger
down the bridge of my nose.
you whisper,
beautiful.
and i can tell you aren't
talking about me physically.
because you're lost in my eyes.
my soul you see.

if i was a kid again i would tell myself this.
don't worry about growing up fast,
it will come so quickly.
just enjoy what you have right now.
your clothes you picked out that don't match.
your endless need to laugh.
your hair is windblown in two braids.
your love for dirt and finding worms.
making sure your little voice is heard.
this time is precious and so short.

i want to get older with you.
i do.
but i want to enjoy
my time with you now.
i am not ready to think about our end.
wrinkling and turning gray.
i want to focus on who we are today.
young and vibrant.
so much life.
anything can happen,
but i am trusting it will all work out
in due time.

i am not worried about
who is watching me.
i will dance anyway.
hands up in the breeze.
either way, they will have something to say.
that i am either too loud or too quiet.
so instead i am being who i truly am.
someone who cares for others,
but doesn't let their negative opinions
make me shine any less.

i'll always save a spot for you
when you are ready to join me.
i'll have a hug for you or two.
but i'll wait until you are ready.

i am convinced that having
so much time to think in my head
created a beautiful imagination.
but it also created the anxiety i now have,
because i think too deeply about
every scenario at hand.

i want to live somewhere
the sun kisses my face daily.
my freckles come to life.
i can eat lunch outside.
take a walk as the birds
sing in the trees.
i want to be in a place
that feels so alive
where it is hard to not believe
there is beauty.

i tell you i don't need flowers,
but you buy them anyway.
i tell you i don't need you to
call and check in,
but you call me anyway.
i tell you i don't need you
to make dinner,
but you make it anyway.
"it isn't about what you need,"
he would say.
"it's about you deserving
to have someone
interested in your day."

we meet for the first time.
i order black coffee.
you order yours with cream.
we talk about the books you like to read.
your face appears calm as you take in me.
there is a silence in between sentences.
but it isn't awkward.
it feels right.
you are looking at me like art.
beauty and depth.
it somehow went from being morning
to being 2 PM.
and it was all so effortless.
falling in love with you.
it didn't feel like we were brand new.
our souls greeting each other again.
eager to catch up on all we missed.

rest in peace to the friendships
that ended without a real reason.
calls became less and less.
time moved on
and you didn't move together.
but you still wish them the best.
you have seen their wedding photos.
they looked beautiful in their dress.
they have a couple of kids now.
you realize you will never know them.
what a beautiful season
you had together when you did.
rest in peace to the friendships
that were a season that was so needed.

i am always ready for spring.
a chance to start new.
grow from what was lost.
prepare to bloom.
spring is the hope i need
that things come back beautifully.

cuddle me, please.
wrap your body around me.
let me know i am needed and wanted.
protected and safe.
i am used to being in arms
that don't care if i run away.

it is one in the morning.
i should be asleep.
but my mind is racing.
it is thinking about all the places
i have gone and what i have said.
it is thinking about all that is to come
and what i don't know yet.
thoughts dancing in my head.
but no one seems to think as deeply as me.
how can we be
on this ball in space spinning?
what does it mean?
it is one in the morning
and i probably won't sleep.

i'll never forget the sunrises and sunsets
that carried me through the days
where i didn't think light would come
in such a beautiful way.

and i would like to think that
my love for you
will always be like a garden.
some seasons
there will be
more growth in the soil
than there is sprouting from the seeds.

we are at the beach.
you look over at me.
the sun's in your eyes
so you are squinting.
i count the freckles on your face.
1, 2, 3, 4, 5.
i could keep going.
get lost in time.
you tell me the sun's shining
just for us today.
that it's our world.
if we close our eyes,
everyone goes away.
and it's love.
real true love.

you let me know
that saying no was more than ok.
that i didn't have to be sorry for everything.
that i didn't need to apologize for taking up space.
that people looking at me isn't something
i should be afraid of anymore.
you let me know all of this
but were gentle with me
not believing you at first.

i once heard that humming
calms you down
when you are anxious.
so i hummed a lot
and you thought it was because
i was at peace.
but i was on my last straw
of trying to figure out how
to not have anxiety.

i want fresh flowers on the table every sunday.
i want clean sheets and fluffed pillows.
i want a face mask and a bubble bath.
i want the counters of the kitchen to be clean.
but i also recognize that it may not happen.
some weeks the flowers will be wilted.
the sheets wrinkled.
a quick shower will have to do.
the kitchen will have dishes that have piled up
from when i cooked food.
some weeks will not be perfect.
some weeks will be one
i am just happy i made it through.

vulnerability, oh how i fear you.
sharing my soul.
my deepest thoughts.
airing out my dirty laundry.
but what i realized
is that it wasn't me afraid of vulnerability.
it was me afraid of the people
who couldn't handle the raw emotion.
i could tell a stranger
how i was actually feeling
better than someone
i had long known.

i love homemade things.
breads.
jellies.
blankets.
hats.
i love the beauty that comes
from creating with your hands.
but i have to admit i am not
the most patient person
when it comes to creating these things.
i like to do things in a hurry.
but creativity forces you to slow down
if you don't want a mess on your hands.

it is friday.
your best friend comes over
in her sweatpants.
you order pizza and wings.
you catch up on the week
and belly laugh.
she is the one who has seen you
through everything.
braided your hair while you cried.
always the first one you call.
with good or bad news.
she is honest with you.
leave him.
move on.
you deserve better.
it is friday.
you realize as you eat dinner
and drink wine together,
that your best friend
is the one who has
always gotten you through
life's ever-changing weather.

and at the end of the day,
i know you were just trying your best.
you too were still living life for the first time.
you too were trying to figure out how to get it right.
you too had things that weighed you down.
at the end of the day,
i forgive you because
you were still trying to figure out
what it means to be found.

i'll bake you a cake from scratch.
i can't promise it will be the best.
but it will be made with love.
neither of which the child in you
experienced much of.

i am soft with people.
i allow them to slowly open up.
to find out i am not critical of them.
that i come with no judgment.
i know what it feels like
to be met with such harshness.
rigidness and doubt.
i am soft with people
because i am hard on myself.

you used to ask for time to speed up,
but here you are today.
the people you love getting older.
the friends are busy with their own lives.
people are asking when you will have kids,
but you feel like you are still a kid yourself.
how did it all happen so fast?
time moved slowly for so long
and now it won't stop speeding up.

i don't know if it is forever,
but it is now.
and i will appreciate that.
instead of thinking about
all that could happen next.

i don't want to even think about
all the time i have wasted
by consuming what other people are doing.
not giving myself the same
attention and space.
but some days it is easier
to consume than create.

i'm sorry i haven't answered
your texts or calls.
it's not because i don't want to talk to you.
i'm just loving being alone with myself.
it has taken me a long time to get here.
where i'm not avoiding my thoughts
by staying busy
or always having someone near.

he is beautiful.
oh my god, it is true.
he is home
and sunshine.
he is all good things
and i am deserving of this.
i am.

you once had a boy say
the stars shine for you,
while simultaneously
he was always in a bad mood.
you stopped believing
what he said was true.
now you have a boy
that smiles at you
when the stars come out.
but you look up
and he looks at you.
silent but taking you in.
he is at a loss for words
trying to tell you
where his love for you begins.

our favorite book is being made
into a movie.
i wonder if you know
or if that news made you
think of me too.
i probably won't watch it
because it would be hard to get through.
or should this be the olive branch i extend
to have a chance of you back in my life again?

stop wishing for the warmth to come,
because when it does
you will be wishing for cool air instead.
and soon you will find yourself wishing
for everything except what you have right now.

i don't need to know
the purpose anymore.
i am just going to be here
embracing each day.
the sunshine.
the raindrops.
talking with strangers along the way.
i don't need to know
the why or the how.
i am just loving
what i have right now.

you are in a coffee shop.
a stranger sits down
at the table next to you.
you can tell they want to chat.
but you brought work here
and soon you need to head back.
they tell you that they
come here at least once a week.
not because they enjoy the coffee but,
they are waiting for someone to take a seat.
across from them, the chair is empty.
they look at it with hope.
you make your way to the vacant seat.
giving them a bit of your time before you go home.
"*thank you,*" they say.
"*it is easy to feel so alone these days.*"

it's spring.
but it's still a little cold.
i'm wearing your old sweatshirt
from back home.
it doesn't fit as baggy
as they told me it should be.
that's because you aren't
double the size of me.
we are even in our weight.
so your sweatshirt that fits her baggy
fits me great.
why's that not ok?

i often find myself
not wanting to drift too far from home.
the comfort i need when alone.
the place i feel most at peace.
everything is curated for me.
and when i am gone too long
i get a little anxious.
my home is the only place
i feel needed.

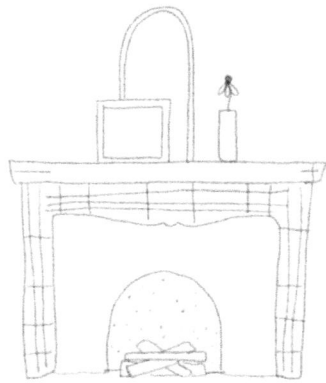

it has been five years,
but i still think about you.
our time together ended too soon.
but now you found the love of your life,
and i am wondering
what could have come of us
if we hadn't parted ways that night.

hope returns.
slowly but surely.
the world stops feeling so heavy.
you don't doubt every word you hear.
you start noticing the small
beautiful things again.
hope comes back
just as darkness
feels like it has settled in.

i told you i loved you at 1 AM.
i was bolder then.
and no i don't regret it.
but it was a vulnerable moment for me.
to open up and share
that i love you so easily.

i wasn't always this quiet you know.
i used to talk louder
and be the first
to volunteer my thoughts.
my diary wasn't the only one to hear
what was dancing in my head.
i used to talk about my pain
and not hide it instead.
but somewhere along the way,
i stopped letting my voice be heard.
i am trying to find her again,
but i am being gentle with her.

it is late at night.
you call me for the third time.
sorry my phone died.
but you sound unsure
if you should believe me.
i promise i want to talk to you.
i am just not used to it being so easy.
usually, i am the one chasing.
calling.
texting.
wondering with no answer.
it is a shock to my system to have someone
who is equally if not more
interested in me.

come be cozy.
grab a mug.
fill it with a warm drink
that you love.
take a deep breath.
maybe your first one all day.
come be cozy.
you deserve a safe place.

i won't let the novelty
wear off anymore.
i want to stay excited about what i have.
not forget how hard i worked
to get to where i stand.
i move on so quickly to the next thing.
i haven't fully appreciated
what i worked so hard to achieve.

while you talk to me on the phone
i doodle flowers on the page.
now taking up the space
where i used to anxiously scribble
while i waited for him to call back.
drunk.
lost.
forgetting what i mean to him.
but you helped me turn
the scribbles into art again.

i never want to hear you
say my real name.
it just doesn't hit the same.
babe.
i'm a nickname kind of girl
and you are a boy with
a plentiful number of
kind names for me.

"you're sorta cute,"
you tell me like we are children again.
a smirk on your face.
i take notice.
we are supposed to be
just friends.
but i think i will never be able to
only see you like that in the end.
and you know it too.
it is time for our relationship
to bloom into something new.

i want to start my day
by saying everything is beautiful.
it might not feel true.
but the more i say it
the more it has the opportunity to.

your number is the only one i remember
somehow when i am drunk
and borrow a phone.
i call you slurring my words.
you ask where i am and if i am alone.
i tell you i am not sure.
i tell you i miss you.
that i can't remember the last time
i didn't feel numb.
you sigh on the other line.
you say you miss me too.
at least i think it is what you said.
i am drunk.
it is hard to clearly hear you.
but then there is a woman's voice
coming from your line.
i tell you i shouldn't have called.
you ask me to wait.
but i hit the end-call button.
wipe a tear from my face.
i am drunk at the bar
that used to be our favorite place.

every trip that i take
makes me appreciate home in a new way.
the routine i have created.
the familiarity around me.
the way i know exactly
where the floorboards creek.
it is comforting to be in a place
where you know all the sounds
and your jumpy mind can take a break.

i don't know how to make
the world as a whole a better place.
but i am starting with my neighbor
and the stranger in line behind me at the store.
i will smile at them more.
compliment their shirt or hair.
give them a second more of my time.
i am moving fast everywhere.
so i slow down.
be more intentional.
i can't make the whole world a better place,
but i am doing my best to not contribute
to it being a scary space.

if you can stop and notice
the sunset hues,
the colors of the leaves
starting to turn,
the birds flying in flocks,
or the gentle breeze on your walk.
you are my kind of person.

i want an afternoon with you.
mac and cheese for lunch.
we share a cookie.
neither of us is in a rush.
i play you my favorite song.
you listen with your full attention.
how beautiful is an afternoon
with both of us fully present?

meet me
for dessert
always.

maybe you were the speed bump
i needed to slow me down.
because i was tumbling fast.
a wrecking ball.
and you were peaceful.
and took your time.
you preferred the back roads
even if the highway traffic was fine.

you weren't at the bar
or the library.
the club
or the hiking trail.
you weren't anywhere.
i was convinced.
i wasn't just going to bump into you
when shopping at the store.
or as we both exit the same door.
our hands wouldn't brush each other
as we reached for the same drink.
i am starting to think
the no-effort approach
isn't going to work.
but i am tired of the search.

you are the most beautiful thing
to come from june.
just as the summer sun starts to bloom.
the light comes later from the moon.
you are exactly what the world could use.

we take a polaroid photo.
you make a silly face.
i hang it up on my mirror
in the perfect place.
i can't remember
the last time i felt this way.
the butterflies in my stomach.
waiting for you to text.
wondering what tomorrow will look like.
could this be it?
will this be the last time
i have to give my whole life story
and not have it go to waste?
please oh please,
i hope you feel the same way.

a year from now may be the same.
and that is a little comforting in a way.
but a little scary too.
a year from now i could be
where i am right now
or somewhere else brand new.

i want to go to the farmer's market
on saturday morning.
get a loaf of fresh baked bread.
the air has just a little chill in it.
i wear a cozy cardigan.
the sun hits my face.
it feels like my perfect day.

*stop and smell
the sunflowers*

"i am breaking up with you."
were the most freeing words.
i wish i could say right then i knew.
so i wouldn't have cried tears at that time.
it was a blessing in disguise.

i will sit and wait
for the cookies to be done.
chocolate chip.
my favorite ones.
because i no longer tell myself
that sugar is too much.
that it is bad.
enough.
i can enjoy the cookies now
without guilt.
the stress about eating it is much worse
than what eating a cookie could do.

someone called me shy again.
you look at me with a smirk on your face.
you tell them i am anything but shy.
that sometimes i get so excited
i talk louder than i need to.
that i tell stories that engage people.
that i am full of words and life.
that the only time i am quiet
is when i am sleeping at night.
and even then i snore a bit.
you tell them that i am anything but shy.
they just haven't truly gotten to know me yet.

i don't know for sure what i believe,
but i will tell you this-
i think the end
is just the start of
all the good there is
to come next.

someone will want to paint you.
write poetry about you.
just remember that
when you are with someone
who acts like
the bare minimum is
too much for them.

you are growing so beautifully.
don't compare your garden and your seeds
to the one who is next to you
growing with ease.
we all grow differently.

i hope to leave you with this.
when you are stressed
and overwhelmed
find the coziness.
the small moment or thing
that brings you peace.
the blanket.
the cup of tea.
take time for yourself.
you deserve rest.
and if the day isn't going great
let it be what it is
and know that you have the next.

and with you it is cozy

to read more work by jennae cecelia,
check out her other twelve books:

don't hurry to tomorrow

meet me at golden hour

healing for no one but me

the sun will rise and so will we

the moon will shine for us too

losing myself brought me here

dear me at fifteen

i am more than my nightmares

uncaged wallflower- extended edition

i am more than a daydream

uncaged wallflower

bright minds empty souls

about the author

www.JennaeCecelia.com

@JennaeCecelia on all social media

jennae cecelia is a best-selling author
of inspirational poetry books
and is best known for her books,
the sun will rise and so will we
and *healing for no one but me*.

she is also an inspirational speaker
who digs into topics like
self-love, self-care, mental health,
and body positivity.

her mission is to encourage people
to reach their full potential and
live a life filled with positivity and love.

would you like a custom poem
written by jennae for you?
she is now offering them on her website.

www.jennaececelia.com/shop-2/p/custom-
poem-request

Made in the USA
Las Vegas, NV
21 October 2024

10174741R00066